· C R E A T I V E   C R A F T S ·

FUN WITH
FABRIC

· JULIET BAWDEN ·

NOTE TO PARENTS

Most projects in this book are easy for children to complete themselves, but your help may be needed when the design calls for a difficult type of stitch or for cutting out especially intricate shapes.

Some projects involve the use of scissors, needle and pins, or a hot iron. Parental supervision is advised in these cases. Please discuss safety with your children, and note in advance which projects will require your supervision.

ACKNOWLEDGMENTS

Projects made by Jan Bridge
and Anne Sharples
Photographs by David Johnson
Illustrations by Joanna Venus

HAMLYN CHILDREN'S BOOKS
Series Editor : Anne Civardi
Series Designer : Anne Sharples
Production Controller : Linda Spillane

First American edition, 1994

Library of Congress Cataloging-in-Publication Data
Bawden, Juliet.
Fun with fabric / Juliet Bawden.
p.   cm. — (Creative crafts)
Summary: Provides instructions on how to make things with fabric,
including pom-poms, tie-dye t-shirts, and rag dolls
ISBN 0-679-83494-X (pbk.) — ISBN 0-679-93494-4 (lib. bdg)
1. Textile crafts — Juvenile literature. 2. Textile painting — Juvenile literature.
[1. Textile crafts. 2. Handicraft.]
I. Title. II. Series: Creative crafts (New York, N.Y.)
TT699.B38 1994
746—dc20   92-51070

Manufactured in Italy

10 9 8 7 6 5 4 3 2 1

CONTENTS

MATERIALS, TIPS, AND HINTS

This book shows you how to make wonderfully original things using different types of fabric. It gives you ideas on how to decorate fabric with special fabric paints, felt-tip pens, glitter, and puff paints, as well as sequins, sparkles, buttons, and beads.

For many of the projects you can use scraps of fabric you can find around the house, but for some you may need to buy bigger pieces of fabric. The special techniques include simple appliqué, tie-dyeing, easy weaving, and printing on fabric with vegetables and spaghetti.

Things to collect and save

Scraps of plain or patterned fabric
Scraps of brightly colored felt
Old buttons
Colored ribbon and string
Sequins and beads
Stiff cardboard or posterboard
Embroidery thread in
   different colors
Small balls of yarn
Old baseball caps
   or berets
Old blue jeans

4

HANDY HINTS

Making things can be messy. Before you start, put sheets of old newspaper on the floor. Remember to pick up pins, needles, and scissors when you have finished.

Wash your paintbrushes after you have used them, and store them in a pot with the bristles pointing upward.

A ruler is useful for measuring and drawing and cutting straight lines. Use tailor's chalk to mark lines on the fabric.

Useful tips

1. You will need a big pair of scissors for cutting big pieces of fabric, and a small pair for small delicate things. Be very careful when you are using them.

2. It is useful to have a pair of pinking shears. They are good for cutting out shapes from fabrics and trimming the ends of ribbons.

3. There are many kinds of special fabric paints and pens. You can find them in craft stores. Try experimenting with puff paints and glitter paints too.

4. If you are printing or dyeing fabric, wear an apron to keep your clothes clean. It is also a good idea to wear rubber gloves so your hands don't get stained with dye.

5. Remember to put tops and lids back on paints and glue to keep them from drying out. Wash any glue off your fingers so that you don't leave dirty finger marks.

6. If you want the things you make to look extra fancy, sew or glue on sequins, ribbons, sparkles, beads, and buttons. You can find these decorations in most department stores.

PAINTED PILLOWCASES

Have you ever thought of designing your
own pillowcase for your bed? All you need is
a solid-colored pillowcase and some fabric
felt-tip pens. Cover it with stars or moons
that will never wash out, like the one below,
or design your own pattern. You can also try
drawing a picture of yourself fast asleep on
your duvet cover or sheet.

Look at your
pajamas or
nightgown to
get an idea
of how to
paint a
picture of
yourself.

Things you need

Plain pillowcase,
  duvet cover, or sheet
Thin cardboard
Pencil or chalk
Scissors
Small sponge or toothbrush
Fabric felt-tip pens
  (including a black one)
Newspaper and masking tape

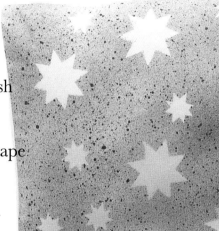

Try dabbing
lots of different
colors onto your
pillowcase.

Seeing stars

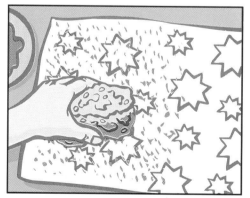

1. Draw seven large star shapes
and ten smaller ones on some
thin cardboard. Carefully cut
them out with small scissors. Put
newspaper in the pillowcase to
keep the paints from running.

2. Arrange the stars on one side
of the pillowcase. Then, with a
small sponge or toothbrush, dab
or splatter fabric paint around the
shapes. Let the paint dry before
you decorate the other side.

3. Use different colors on top of
each other to get a really bright
effect. Let the paints dry and then
take out the newspaper. Turn the
pillowcase inside out and iron it
to set the color.

6

HANDY HINTS

To keep the pillowcase still while you are drawing on it, tape it across the corners to a table or the floor.

Your pictures will look much neater if you draw in one direction with the fabric felt-tip pens.

Instead of using fabric felt-tips, you can use fabric paint. The pens are easier to use, but the paint will go further. For big areas, dab on paint with a sponge.

Counting sheep pillowcase

A body in your bed

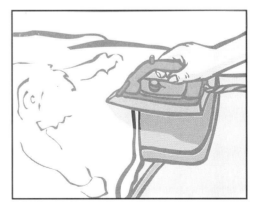

1. Put a white duvet cover on the floor and put flat sheets of newspaper inside it. Lie on top of the duvet with your arms stretched out. Ask a friend to draw around you with a soft pencil or chalk.

2. Stand up carefully. Make sure the shape is exactly how you want it to be. Then slowly go over the outline with a black fabric felt-tip pen. Add details, such as hair, a face, clothes, or pajamas.

3. Fill in the design with colored fabric felt-tip pens or fabric paints. Let it dry and then take out the newspaper. Turn the duvet cover inside out and iron it to set the color.

POTATO PRINT SHORTS

You may have already printed with cut-out potato shapes and paint on paper. Why not use the same idea to brighten up your boxer shorts or pants? Instead of using poster paint, you will need special fabric paint and some big potatoes or carrots to cut up into different patterns.

Things you need

Solid-colored shorts or pants
Fabric paint and a paintbrush
Felt-tip pen
Small vegetable knife
Newspaper and masking tape
Potatoes and carrots

Glue uncooked pieces of spaghetti onto a piece of thick cardboard. Brush paint over them and print lines over the potato prints.

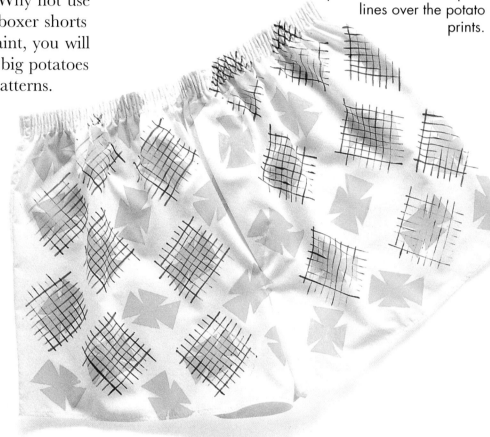

Use different-sized potatoes to make big and small shapes of the same design.

Printed boxer shorts make good presents.

8

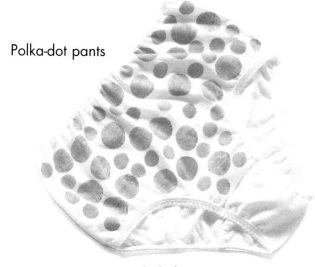

Polka-dot pants

Hearts and kisses

1. Carefully cut a big potato in half, widthways. Draw a big "X" on one half with a felt-tip pen. Cut around the X and cut away the rest of the potato so that the X stands out, as shown.

2. Stuff a pair of boxer shorts with newspaper to keep the paint from running through. Tape the shorts to a tabletop or the floor. Dab the cut potato with a tissue to mop up any extra potato juice.

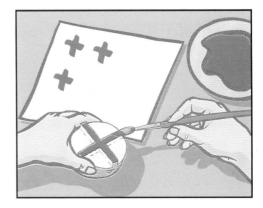

3. Brush paint onto the potato cut-out. Turn the potato over and print the pattern onto some paper to test it. If it looks good, print as many Xs as you want onto the boxer shorts.

4. Now cut a different pattern out of the other half of the big potato, such as a diamond or heart shape, as shown. Brush a different color paint onto the heart and print this pattern on the shorts.

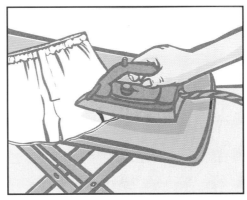

5. When the prints are dry, turn the shorts over and print on the back. Let the shorts dry. Then turn them inside out. Iron the shorts on the inside to set the color.

6. You can use carrots to print polka dots in lots of different colors. Cut off the top and brush paint onto the cut end. Use big carrots to print big dots, and little carrots for small dots.

9

COOL CAPS

These two pages show you how to make plain hats, caps, or berets look extra special. There are lots of ideas on how to decorate them with studs, puff paint, and fancy sparkles and sequins. You can also cover them with all sorts of bright felt shapes.

Fruit-salad beret

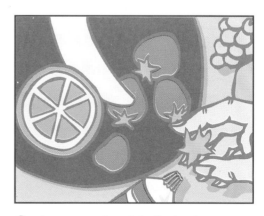

Things you need

Cap, felt beret, or straw hat
Sparkles and studs
Puff paints
Colored felt
Scissors
Fabric glue
Ribbon or ribbon rosebuds
Tracing-paper
Black felt-tip pen
Paper and pencil
Pins

Flower-power hat

Fruit-salad beret

1. To make this fruit-salad beret, first draw your design on paper. Draw any fruit you like, such as strawberries, oranges, grapes, and bananas.

2. Trace over the design and cut out each shape from the tracing-paper. Pin the tracing-paper shapes to the felt and cut them out.

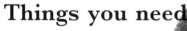

3. Arrange the felt fruit shapes on the top of the beret. Pin them in place. One by one put glue on the back of each shape and glue it down.

10

Puff-paint cap

Use a simple design, such as squiggles and dots, when you decorate a cap with puff paint. To make the paint puff up faster, heat it with a hair dryer.

Sparkling studs

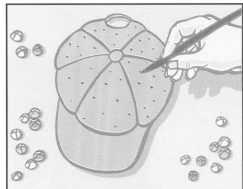

Before you start, mark the hat with a felt-tip pen to show where you want the studs to go. Push each stud from the front to the back of the cap, then close it.

Flower power

To make a pretty hat, cover a straw or felt hat with felt flowers, bows, or ribbon rosebuds. Glue or sew them around the brim of the hat.

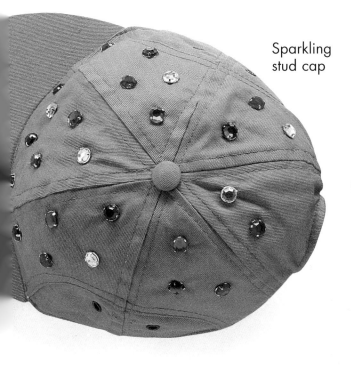

Sparkling stud cap

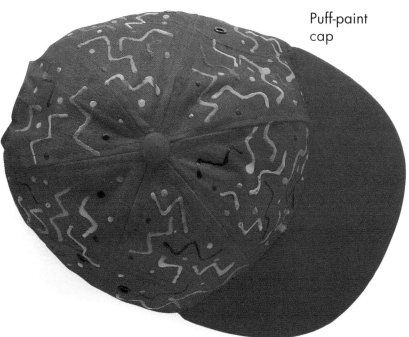

Puff-paint cap

HANDY HINTS

The prongs on studs are sometimes difficult to close. Try pushing each prong down with the blades of a pair of closed scissors.

When you are decorating a hat with felt shapes, arrange the shapes and pin them into position before you glue them down.

GLOW-IN-THE-DARK BANNERS

Make glow-in-the-dark banners to hang up in your bedroom. All you need is some black fabric and some special fluorescent fabric paints. You can decorate the banners with spooky monsters and ghosts, or design a super space scene. The paints will glow for up to twenty minutes in the dark. To make them glow again just turn on the light for a few seconds.

Things you need

Black paper and white and colored chalks
One yard of black fabric
Fluorescent fabric paints
Newspaper and masking tape
Fabric glue
Ribbon or string
Two thin dowels, each
   about 18 in. long

Glow-in-the-dark
night scene

Spage-age banner

1. Before you begin, draw your design on black paper, using colored chalk. Tape the black fabric to a tabletop. Copy your design onto the fabric with white chalk, as shown.

2. Go over the outline of your design with fluorescent paints. Fill in any details. Squeeze the tubes very gently so that the paint comes out slowly. Let the paint dry.

3. If you want to make your banner extra fancy, add fake beady eyes, sequins, or sparkles. To stick eyes on, put blobs of paint on the fabric and press the eyes into the paint.

HANDY HINTS

Glow-in-the-dark fabric paint usually comes in a plastic tube with a nozzle. Do not press too hard, or the paint will come out too fast and your designs may smudge.

It is a good idea to have paper towels or rags handy to catch any drips while you are painting.

If you want to cover a large area with paint, spread it on with a piece of cardboard or a flat ice-cream stick.

Make glow-in-the-dark badges to sew on your jacket or jeans.

Space-age banner

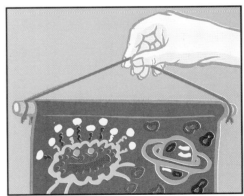

4. To make the banner, turn the sides of the fabric under by about ½ in. Stick them down with fabric glue. Lay the fabric face down and put one dowel near the top edge, as shown.

5. Roll the fabric around the dowel and glue it down firmly with fabric glue, as shown. Glue the second dowel to the bottom edge of the banner in the same way.

6. When the glue is dry, cut a piece of ribbon a little longer than the width of your banner. Tie the ends to the top dowel, as shown. Hang the banner up in your bedroom and watch it glow.

13

REALLY RAG DOLL

Here is a rag doll with a real difference. You can make it without any sewing at all. All you need are lots of colorful strips of fabric, string or yarn, and a ball for the doll's head. It makes a very good present to hang on the wall or just to decorate someone's bed.

Things you need

White, red, and patterned fabric
Yarn, string, or thin ribbon
Small, soft ball
Scissors

Strips of fabric	
Head/Body	7 white strips 1 in. x 27 in.
Arms	16 strips 1 in. x 8 in.
Skirt	19 strips 1 in. x 24 in.
Bodice	1 long red strip 1½ in. x 44 in.
Scarf	1 red square 9 in. x 9 in.

Really rag girl doll

Rag girl

1. Cover the ball with the white strips of fabric, three across and four in the other direction. Twist the strips at the neck and tie them together with yarn.

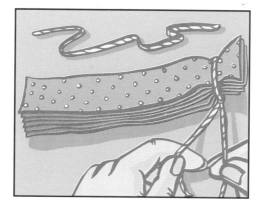

2. Make a long bundle out of all the arm strips, as shown. Tie a piece of yarn about 1 in. from each end, to hold the strips of fabric together.

3. Divide the white neck strips in half. Put the arms between them. Tie yarn around the white strips, as shown, to hold in the arms at the waist.

14

Baby rag doll

Really rag boy doll

Rag boy

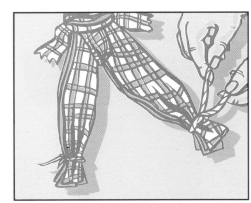

4. Tie another piece of string loosely around the waist. Loop the skirt strips over it, one at a time. When they are placed evenly around the doll, tighten the string.

5. For a scarf, fold the square in half and tie it around the doll's head. Wrap the bodice strip around the neck, cross it over at the front, and tie it at the back.

For a boy doll, divide the skirt strips in half. Leave one in the middle. Tie each half with yarn. Tuck the middle strip between the legs and loop it over the waist tie.

15

AMAZING ANGELS

On these two pages you can find out how to make angels out of scraps of cloth. They make wonderful decorations to hang on a Christmas tree, or just to hang on a wall. Instead of making an angel, you can leave the wings off to make a little cloth doll.

Things you need

½ yard of fabric
Yellow or patterned fabric
   for the dress
Paper and pencil
Scissors
Pins, needle, and thread
Red and black felt-tip pens
Polyester fill
Embroidery thread
Thin ribbon

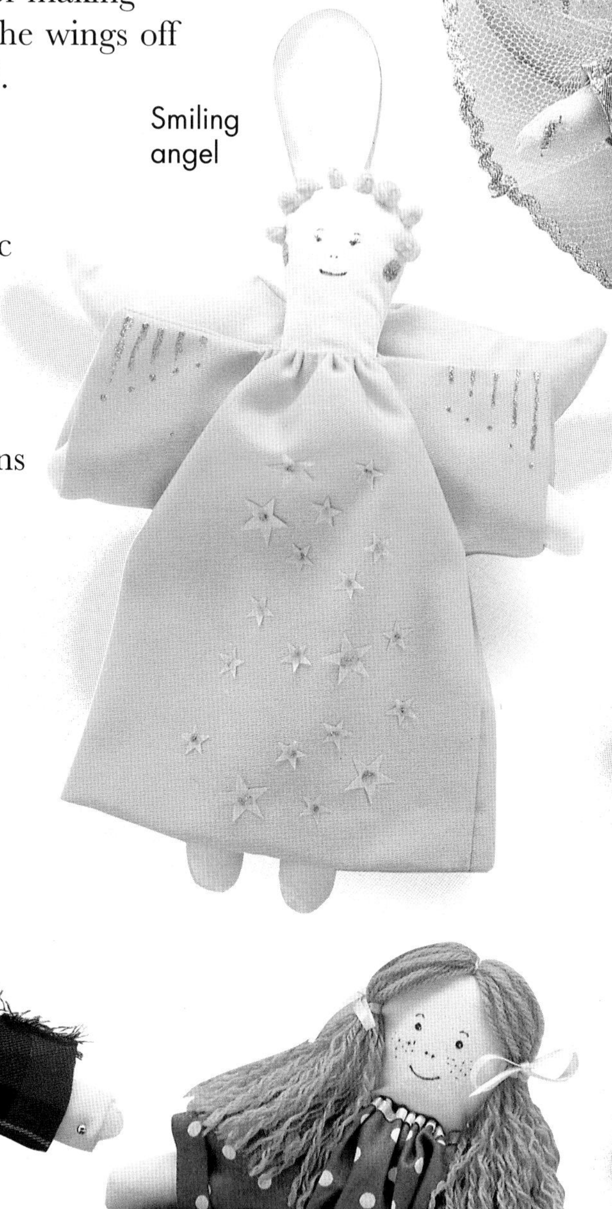

Smiling angel

Make a big angel for the top of a Christmas tree.

Make different-colored angels.

Without the wings, the angels turn into little cloth dolls.

16

Smiling angel

1. Draw a simple doll shape, about 6 in. high, on a piece of paper. Draw a wing shape, 7 in. long. Draw a ½ in. seam allowance all around the shapes. These are your patterns.

2. Cut out the patterns. Fold the fabric in half and pin the patterns to it. Cut them out so you have two fabric doll shapes and two fabric wing shapes. Take out the pins.

3. With the right sides facing, pin the doll shapes together and the wings shapes together. Sew around the edges. Leave a gap in the body and the wings as shown. Turn the fabric right side out.

4. Fill both the body and the wings with polyester fill. Sew up the gaps. Draw a **T** shape, as shown, on paper big enough to fit the angel's body. This is the dress pattern. Cut it out.

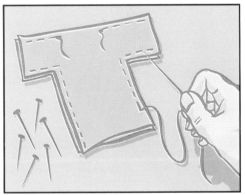

5. Fold the dress fabric in half and pin the pattern to it. Cut out two dress shapes. With the right sides facing, sew along the shoulders and down the sides. Turn the dress right side out.

6. Slip the dress on the angel. Gather in the neck and neaten all the edges. Sew on the wings and a ribbon loop. Draw on a face. Make the hair by sewing on tiny knots of embroidery thread.

HANDY HINTS

When you are making the angel's body pattern, make the head connect to the body without a neck. This makes it easier to turn the angel right side out.

To make an angel that glitters, sew or glue sequins and sparkles onto the clothes.

If you don't have any polyester fill for stuffing, you can use tissues, cotton balls, or scraps of material instead.

Instead of making the hair out of embroidery thread, you can make long hair out of strands of yarn, and short hair out of furry material.

TERRIFIC TIE-DYE

Now you can make your own special tie-dye T-shirts covered with crazy, one-of-a-kind designs. All you need is a T-shirt, strong string, and fabric dyes. The great thing about tie-dye is that no two designs are ever the same!

Things you need

Light-colored T-shirt
Bucket and water
Cold-water fabric dye
Wooden spoon
Salt
Strong string
Vinegar

Wacky tie-dye T-shirts

Tie-dye T-shirt

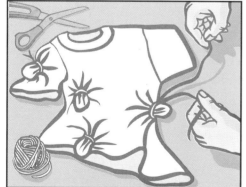

1. Wash and dry the T-shirt you are going to tie-dye. Clump together a little section of the shirt and tie it with strong string. Make a very tight knot. Make little clumps all over the shirt.

2. Put on the apron and rubber gloves. Follow the instructions on the packet of dye. Often the dye is first dissolved separately in warm water. Adding salt will create deeper colors.

3. Fill the bucket with water. Pour the dye mixture into the bucket. Stir the dye. Drop the T-shirt into the bucket of dye and push it down. Keep stirring it for about ten minutes.

18

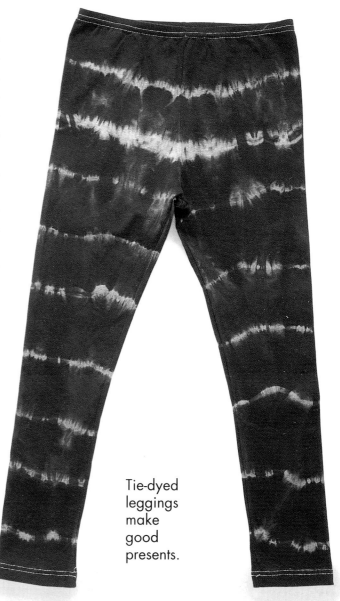

Tie-dyed leggings make good presents.

Tie-dye a long piece of fabric to make a swirly scarf.

4. Make sure that the T-shirt is completely covered with dye and leave it. Stir from time to time. After fifty minutes, take it out and rinse it under cold water until the water runs clear.

5. Hang the T-shirt up to dry. When it is dry, undo the clumps of fabric. Now you can see the cool patterns all over the T-shirt. The best results usually come from small, tight clumps.

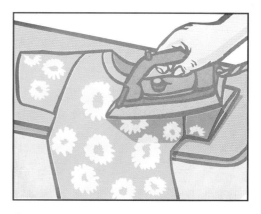

6. Iron the shirt to take out the wrinkles the knots have made. To preserve the colors longer, wash the shirt with a little vinegar before you wear it.

RECYCLED RAGS

Do your favorite jeans have holes in them?
Instead of mending them with plain
patches, you can design your own fabric
pictures to patch them with. All you need
are scraps of fabric and some colorful
embroidery thread.

Things you need

Blue jeans, a skirt, or shorts
Scraps of fabric
Pins, needle, and strong thread
Embroidery thread
Scissors

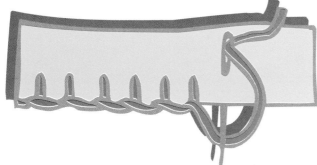

Make a patch
pocket and
sew it onto
your skirt.

Embroider
your initials
on your
blue jeans.

Blanket stitch

1. Work from left to right with the thread at the top
edge of the fabric. Point the needle upward and push
it through the fabric from front to back, as shown.

2. Pull the thread out between the fabric and the
thread, as shown. Do this again and again until you
have sewn along all the edges of the fabric shape. Try
not to pull the thread too tight.

Before you sew on the patches, draw your design on paper.

Try to find fabric decorated with pictures of animals or flowers. Cut them out and sew them onto your jeans.

If you don't like sewing, stick the shapes onto your jeans using an iron and fusible interfacing. This method is not as strong as sewing but it is very effective.

Pretty patches

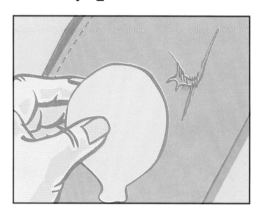

1. Measure the hole that needs patching. Then cut out a shape, like this big round balloon. Make it a little bigger than the hole so there is enough fabric to fold over for a neat hem.

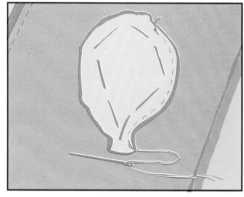

2. Pin the shape over the hole and sew it down with large basting stitches. Take out the pins. Then fold under the edges of the patch, and sew it down with small running stitches, as shown.

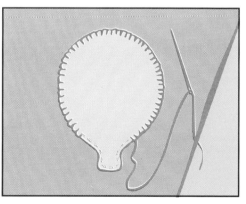

3. Decorate and neaten the edges with blanket stitch as shown in the box on the facing page. It is best to use doubled embroidery thread, as shown.

4. Add more shapes, such as a person or an animal. Sew them using stitches from steps two and three. Remove the basting stitches when you are done.

BEAUTIFUL BAGS

Instead of buying an expensive bag, why not
make one for yourself? You can easily turn an
old pair of blue jeans into a stunning shoulder
bag decorated with felt, sequins, beads, or
paints. Out of scraps of fabric, make a neck
purse to carry money and other important
things.

Things you need
for a blue jeans bag

Old blue jeans
Scissors and tape measure
Pins, needle, and strong thread
Ballpoint pen

for a neck purse

Piece of fabric, 5 in. long
 and 8 in. wide
Narrow ribbon, 30 in. long
Embroidery thread, ribbon, or lace
Needle and thread
Scissors and fabric glue
Fabric paints, buttons, sequins,
 and felt for decoration

Blue jeans bag

Cut out flower
shapes from felt
and sew or glue
them all over the
front of your
bag.

1. Turn the blue jeans inside
out. Draw a line across them,
where the legs meet the body.
Cut along the line. Using a
running stitch, sew along the
bottom, as shown, to make a bag.

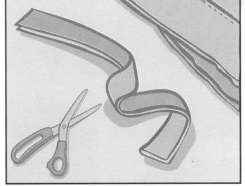

2. To make a shoulder strap for
the bag, cut a strip of material,
about 24 in. x 4 in., from one of
the legs you have cut off. Then
fold the strip of fabric in half
along its length.

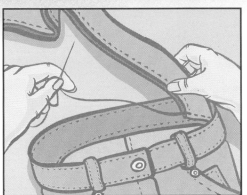

3. Fold over both the edges of
the strap by ½ in. and pin them
together. Sew along the edge.
Then sew the two ends of the
strap onto the inside of the blue
jeans bag at the waist.

Nifty neck purses

Nifty neck purse

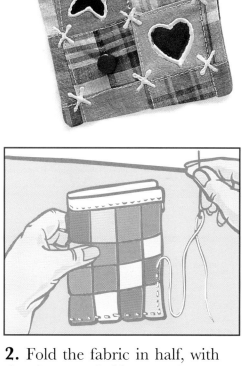

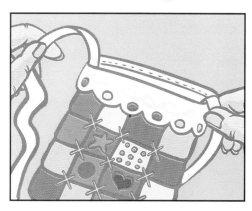

1. With the fabric inside out, turn in the top edge about ¼ in. and sew it down. Turn the fabric over and sew on a thin strip of lace. Decorate the fabric with buttons, puff paint, and felt.

2. Fold the fabric in half, with the decorated sides together. Then sew along the bottom and the open side, about ¼ in. from the edges, so that you have a small purse, as shown.

3. Stitch one end of the narrow ribbon to one side of the purse, close to the top. Stitch the other end to the other side of the purse. Then turn the purse right side out.

EASY WEAVING

These marvelous mats are woven out of yarn. They can be plain, striped, or patterned, and are fun and easy to make with a homemade cardboard loom. You can also weave small coasters for glasses and cups, a bookmark, and even a colorful purse.

Things you need

Cardboard (for the loom)
Ruler and pencil
Scissors
Darning needle
Small balls of yarn (cotton or wool)

HANDY HINTS

The threads that go up and down are called the warp. Join them in the center so the knots will be woven in.

The threads that go across are called the weft. Do not pull the weft too tight or the weaving will be uneven.

Make a set of colorful striped mats. Add pretty yarn fringes.

A cardboard loom

1. To make a loom, measure and cut a piece of stiff cardboard slightly larger than you want your mat to be. This loom is 7 in. long and 5 in. wide.

2. Draw two long lines across the cardboard, 1 in. from the top and 1 in. from the bottom. Mark short lines, ½ in. apart. Snip along the short lines to the long lines with small scissors.

3. To thread the loom, tie the end of some yarn to the top left-hand corner. Wind on the warp so that it goes up and down the front of the loom and under the slits, as shown.

How to weave

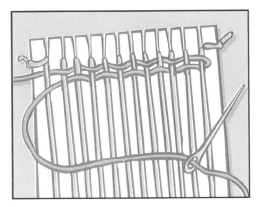 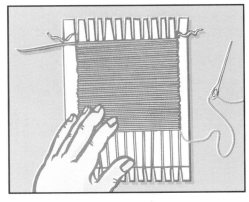 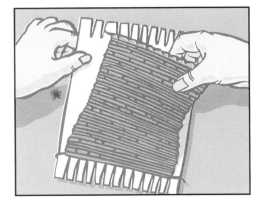

1. Thread the darning needle with yarn and start weaving under and over the threads of the warp. For the next row, weave over the threads you went under, and weave under the ones you went over.

2. Repeat these two rows until you have woven the length of the loom. As you weave, gently push each row close to the one above it to make sure the mat is nice and tight.

3. When you have reached the bottom of the loom, cut off the remaining yarn, and knot or glue down the end. Then carefully lift the mat off the loom so that you can use the loom again.

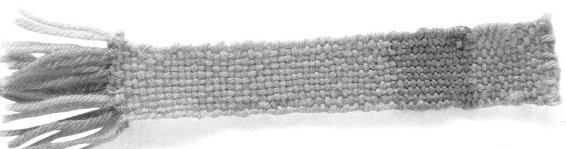

Weave some yarn into a big bright bookmark.

Striped mats

To make a purse, wind the warp thread onto the back and front of the loom. Weave first on the front of the loom and then on the back of the loom with the weft yarn doubled.

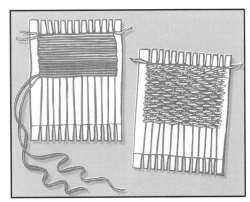

For horizontal stripes, weave five rows in one color and two in another. Weave the color you are not using into the side of the row you are working. To make vertical stripes, weave one row in one color, and the next in another color.

25

SACHET SWEETS

These sweet-smelling lavender bags look like candies. You can make them in different shapes and sizes, out of scraps of plain or patterned fabric. Fill a basket with sachets as a pretty table decoration or put them into drawers to make your clothes smell nice and fresh. If you can't find any lavender, try using dried rose petals or potpourri instead.

Things you need

Scraps of fabric
Dried lavender, rose petals, or
  potpourri
Thin ribbon and thread
Lace or embroidery anglaise
Scissors and pins
Fabric glue

Hang up a row of sweets glued or sewn to some ribbon.

Make big sweets to scent your clothes.

Fill a basket with sachet sweets made from scraps of felt.

To make glittery sweets, use shiny fabric decorated with sequins, sparkles, or glitter paint.

26

Sew a loop of cord on a sachet sweet and hang it over a coat hanger.

HANDY HINTS

It is much easier to make the sachet sweets if you do not fill them too full of lavender or potpourri.

Instead of using thread to tie up the ends of the sweets, you can use colorful rubber bands or yarn.

Sachet sweets

1. Cut out a piece of fabric, about 4 in. wide and 4 in. long. Cut two pieces of narrow ribbon and two strips of lace or embroidery anglaise, each about 4 in. long.

2. Spread glue along the inside of one of the ribbons and one of the strips of lace. Glue them to the right side of the fabric, along one edge, as shown. Do the same on the other edge.

3. When the glue is dry, glue a strip of fabric, about 1½ in. wide and 4 in. long, to the middle of the square piece of fabric, as shown. Instead of fabric you could use a piece of wide ribbon.

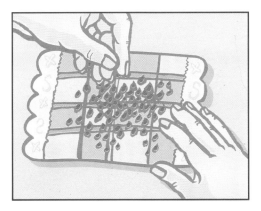

4. Turn the fabric square over and put a small pile of lavender or potpourri in the middle. Then fold in the top and bottom edges so that you have a little sausage shape.

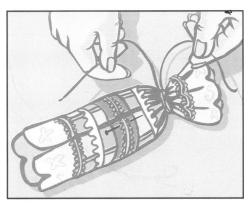

5. Hold the sausage shape together with a pin. Then cut a piece of strong thread and tie it tightly, about 1 in. from one end, as shown, so that it looks like a big candy.

6. Put more lavender in the open end of the sweet if it is not full enough. Tie up the end. Take out the pin and trim off the thread. Then tie a bow of thin ribbon over the thread at each end.

HANDY POT HOLDERS

Oven mitts and gloves make good presents, especially when they look bright and cheerful, like this funny face mitt and slithery snake glove. If you line them with thick batting, you can use them to hold hot pots, plates, and dishes. But be careful not to put them close to a flame or they will burn.

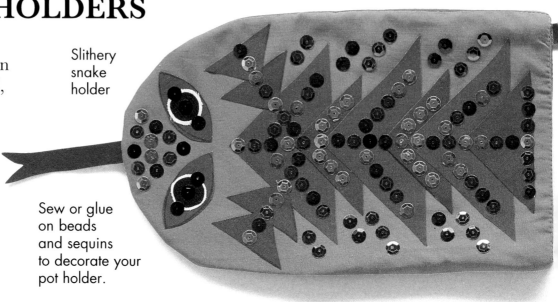

Slithery snake holder

Sew or glue on beads and sequins to decorate your pot holder.

Things you need

Pencil and paper
1 yard of plain fabric
½ yard of thick batting
Scraps of felt
Beads and buttons
Pins, needle, and thread
Scissors
Fabric glue
Ribbon

HANDY HINTS

It is easier to make an oven mitt without a thumb, but it is easier to hold hot things with a mitt that has one.

Make the gap in between the hand and the thumb extra big. Use a pencil to push the thumb the right side out.

To make an oven mitt that is big enough for an adult to wear, draw the pattern around an adult's hand.

Funny face

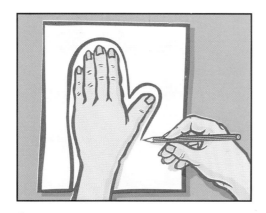

1. Draw around your hand on a sheet of paper, keeping your fingers together. Make the thumb extra big. Cut out the pattern, making it a little bigger than your hand all the way around.

2. Pin the paper pattern to the plain fabric. Cut out four gloves, as shown. Then pin the pattern to the thick batting and cut out two more gloves exactly the same size, as shown.

3. Pin two fabric gloves together with the right sides facing each other. Sew around three sides of the glove, as shown, ¼ in. from the edge. Turn the glove right side out.

Funny
face pot
holder

Try making a
patchwork pot
holder out of lots
of scraps of fabric.

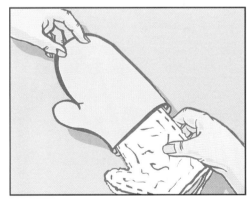

4. Sew a batting glove onto each of the two remaining fabric gloves, as shown. Then, with the fabric gloves facing each other, sew another glove as you did the first one.

5. Keeping the glove inside out, slip it inside the first glove to make a thick lining. Fold in the edges of the inner and outer gloves at the wrist and sew them neatly together.

6. To make a funny face, cut out a felt mouth, eye, and ear and some felt hair. Glue them to the glove. Sew a loop of ribbon with a felt flower onto the bottom so you can hang up the pot holder.

FUNNY FINGER PUPPETS

Turn a pair of gloves into a pirate, a scarecrow, a soldier, a crazy clown, and a happy man. Or design your own finger puppets with animal or spooky fingertips. Make them for yourself or as a present for a friend. Small children will love wearing them.

Things you need

Solid-colored knitted gloves
Scraps of felt and fabric
Yarn, beads, buttons, and ribbon
Scissors, needle, and thread
Fabric glue and tissue paper

Amazing animal puppet

Funny finger people puppet

Finger people

1. For a pirate little finger, cut out a round felt head and a red nose. Cut out a beard, an eye and an eye-patch. Glue the features to the face and glue the face onto the glove.

2. Cut out two felt hats. Glue one to the front of the finger and the other to the back so they cover the top of the head. Decorate the hat and tie a fabric scarf around the neck.

3. Make a scarecrow for the next finger. Cut out felt eyes, a nose, a mouth, and two hats. Glue yarn hair to the head before you glue on the hats. Tie on a scarf.

4. For the soldier on the middle finger, cut out a face, mustache, a nose, and a hat with a chin strap. Sew on four tiny beads to finish off his outfit.

5. Make the clown on the fourth finger with cross-shaped eyes, a nose, a mouth, and a bright peaked hat with a flower. Gather ribbon for his collar and sew buttons below it.

6. The smiling man on the thumb has a shirt and collar, a bowtie, and a felt jacket. Cut out a face, and glue little eyes, a smiling mouth, and fuzzy yarn hair to it.

Make some spooky gloves to wear at Halloween.

HANDY HINTS

To keep the glue from sticking the fingers of the glove together, stuff each one with tissue paper before you start.

Make sure you do not sew the fingers together when you sew on the buttons or other decorations.

Glue the nose, eyes, and mouth to the face before you glue the face to the finger of the glove.

FANCY FEET

With special fabric paints and felt-tip pens you can make your sneakers look almost brand-new, even if they are quite old. If you want them to look extra cool, you can decorate them with strips of shiny sequins. Try painting pictures and patterns on your socks as well, or decorate them with buttons, beads, and tiny bells.

Things you need

Solid-colored sneakers
Solid-colored socks
Fabric paints and pens
Glitter and puff paints
Fabric felt-tip pens
Thin ribbon and
  ribbon bows
Buttons, beads, and bells
Paper and pencil
Newspaper and scissors

For super cool sneakers, use bright metallic ribbon for the shoelaces.

Paint swirls of shiny puff paint on sneakers.

Snazzy sneakers

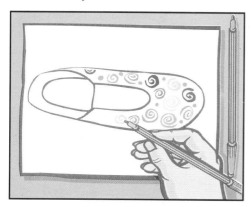

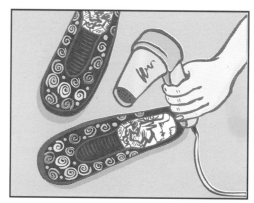

1. Before you start, decide what pattern you are going to paint on your sneakers. It is easier to paint a simple pattern, such as dots, stripes, or squiggles. Draw your design on a sheet of paper.

2. Stuff the sneakers with old newspaper and start painting on the design. Paint one shoe before you start the other, working from the front to the back, as shown. Use lots of different colors.

3. Squeeze little dots of puff paint in between the shiny swirls. Then let the paint dry. Use a hair dryer if you want the paint to dry faster. Then take the newspaper out of the sneakers.

Party
socks

Painted
socks

Jingling
socks

HANDY HINTS

Draw around the sock on a piece of thin cardboard. Cut out the cardboard shape and put it inside the sock when you are using fabric paints or pens, to keep them from running.

It is very easy to sew the front of a sock to the back by mistake. Keep the cardboard shape in the sock while you are sewing.

Stretch the sock as you sew decorations onto it. Otherwise the thread will break when you put the sock on.

Super socks

1. For pretty party socks, sew tiny ribbon roses around the top of plain socks. You can also make tiny bows out of thin, colorful ribbon and sew them onto the top of the socks, as shown.

2. Sew colorful beads around the top of a sock. These should only go as far as the ankle so they do not touch your shoes. If you would like noisy socks, sew on some tiny bells.

3. You can paint patterns on socks, using fabric paints, puff paints, and felt-tip pens. These do not wash off. If you want to make socks sparkle, use special fabric glitter paint as well.

PRETTY POM-POMS

These pretty pom-poms are simple and fun to make and can be any size you like. You can make them from all kinds of yarn and use them to decorate hats, belts, headbands, and gloves. You can also make funny pom-pom people, fluffy animals, and creepy-crawly caterpillars or snakes.

Things you need

Thin cardboard
Pencil
Scissors
Cup or small plate
Small balls of yarn

Cover a headband with sparkly pom-poms.

Sew different kinds of pom-poms together to make a creepy caterpillar.

Pretty pom-pom

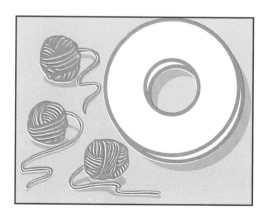

1. Draw two circles on thin cardboard by drawing around a cup or small plate with a pencil. Draw a smaller circle in the middle of each big circle, as shown.

2. Using small scissors, cut out the two big circles of cardboard. Cut out the two small circles in the middle. Put one cardboard ring on top of the other.

3. Wind a long piece of yarn into a ball, small enough to go through the hole in the middle of the rings. Make two or three small balls of yarn, as shown.

Make extra big pom-poms for a woolly hat.

Brighten up your gloves with pretty pom-poms.

Make a chirpy yellow pom-pom chick.

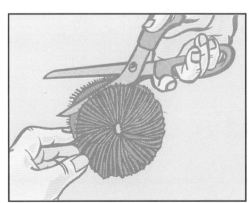

Mixed-up pom-poms

Striped pom-pom
To make striped pom-poms, wind thin layers of different-colored yarn around the cardboard rings, one on top of the other. Use four colors.

Polka-dot pom-pom
For polka-dot pom-poms, wind one layer of your main color yarn around the cardboard rings. Add thin strips, as shown, of another color on every other layer of yarn.

Squared-up pom-pom
For squared pom-poms, divide the rings into four quarters with a pencil. Cover each one with a different-colored yarn.

Sparkly pom-pom
To make a pom-pom that sparkles, you need to buy special yarn that looks as if it is full of tiny pieces of glitter.

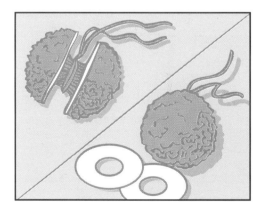

4. Wind the yarn around the two rings, as shown. Keep on winding until the rings are completely covered and only a tiny hole is left in the middle.

5. Then push one blade of the scissors between the two rings, as shown. Cut through all the yarn around the edges. Be careful not to cut the cardboard.

6. Pull the rings slightly apart and wind a long piece of yarn tightly around the middle of the pom-pom. Tie a tight knot. Then carefully pull off the rings.

35

T-SHIRT ART

With a little imagination you can transform a plain white T-shirt into something much more original and fun to wear. Draw on your own design and decorate it with bright fabric paints, special puff paints, sparkling glitter paints, or fabric felt-tip pens.

Things you need

White or solid-
  colored T-shirt
Paper and pencil
Newspaper
Masking tape
Fabric paints, puff
  paints, glitter paints,
  or fabric felt-tip pens
Tailor's chalk or very
  soft pencil
Embroidery transfers
Carbon paper
Iron

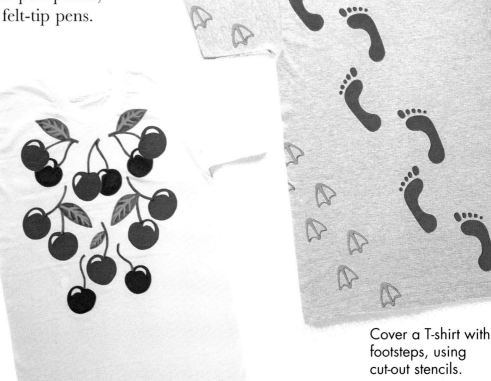

Cover a T-shirt with footsteps, using cut-out stencils.

Embroidery
transfer T-shirt

Carbon-copy T-shirt

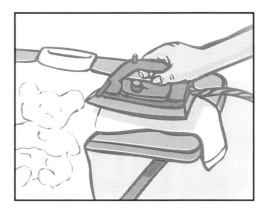

1. Before you start, draw your design on a big sheet of paper. Put a piece of carbon paper, ink side down, onto the front of a T-shirt. Put your design on top and trace over the design.

2. Take off the carbon paper. The design will show up on the shirt. Put sheets of newspaper inside the shirt and color in your design with glitter paint, puff paint, or fabric felt-tip pens.

3. When the paint has dried, take out the newspaper and turn the T-shirt inside out. Iron over the design on the wrong side to set the paint, so it can't be washed out.

36

As a birthday present, give a friend a T-shirt with his or her age on the front.

Carbon-copy T-shirt

HANDY HINTS

To keep the T-shirt from moving while you draw on your design, tape it to a tabletop.

Embroidery transfers usually come in a big sheet with lots of designs, letters, and numbers. It is best to work out your design before you buy them.

Transfer T-shirt

Permanent pictures

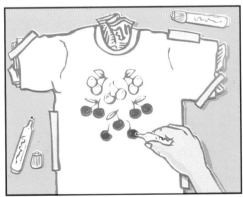

1. Choose and buy the embroidery transfers you want to use for your design. Cut them out. Then tape them, one at a time, to the front of the T-shirt, as shown. Make sure you put them ink side down.

2. Carefully iron over the transfers, using a hot iron. Then remove the paper. The designs will now be on your T-shirt. Color them in with fabric paint, puff paint, glitter paint, or fabric felt-tip pens.

Make a picture on your T-shirt using different techniques, such as drawing, transfers, and stencils. Use different pens and paints. Let them dry before setting them with a hot iron.

QUICK-STICK PENCIL CASE

Make your own pencil case or toiletry bag quickly and easily without any sewing at all. All you need is some vinyl, sticky-backed felt, and some Velcro to keep it closed. You can also design a bigger bag for your swimsuit and towel.

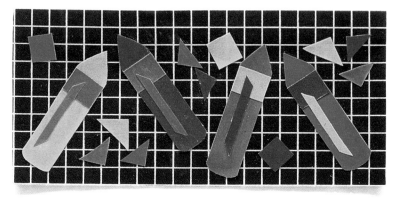

Quick-stick
pencil case

Things you need

Sticky-backed felt
Sticky-backed Velcro, 9 in. long
Fabric glue and ruler
Ballpoint pen or pencil
Vinyl (available at fabric stores)

Make your pencil case longer
if you want to fit in a ruler.

Perfect pencil case

1. Draw two rectangles, each about 9 in. long and 4 in. wide, on the inside of the vinyl. Draw a ½ in. margin around both rectangles, as shown. Cut out the bigger rectangles.

2. Peel the backing paper off a strip of Velcro, 8 in. long. Stick it onto one of the long sides of one of the vinyl pieces. Stick Velcro onto one of the long sides of the second rectangle.

3. To decorate the pencil case, cut out different shapes, such as these crayons, from sticky-backed felt. Stick them onto the back and the front of the outside of the rectangles.

Decorate a beach bag with fish and other sea creatures.

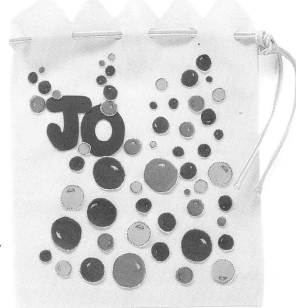

Stick your name onto your toiletry bag.

Laced-up case

Toiletry bag

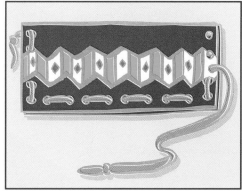

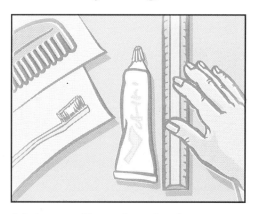

4. Spread glue around the three edges of one of the rectangles, inside out, as shown. Line up the Velcro so they match perfectly. Then stick the two rectangles together to make a pencil case.

As well as gluing the pencil case, you can tie it together with a shoelace to make it even stronger. Use a hole punch around three of the edges and thread the shoelace through the holes, as shown.

Make a toiletry bag in the same way as your pencil case. To work out the size, measure the things you are going to put inside, such as a toothbrush, comb, toothpaste, and shampoo.

JOLLY JUGGLERS

All you need to make these jolly
juggling balls are small pieces of felt
and dried peas, lentils, or rice. Try
making a tossed-salad juggling set
with a tomato, a cucumber, and
green lettuce. Or give a friend
a set of jolly juggler dice.

Things you need

Pencil, paper, and ruler
Scissors and pinking shears
Felt
Pins, needle, and thread
Dried peas, beans, rice, or lentils
Embroidery thread (for decoration)

Make three jolly
juggler dice out
of black, red, and
white felt.

Make jolly
jugglers with
names.

Tossed-
salad set

40

Jolly
jugglers

Jolly jugglers

1. Draw six squares, each 2 in. by 2 in., on paper. Cut out the squares and pin each one to a separate piece of felt. Cut out the felt squares and take out the pins.

2. Sew three different-colored squares of felt together, as close to the edges as possible. Now you have a row of squares, as shown. Do the same with the other three felt squares.

3. Sew the two rows of felt squares together so they form a cube shape, as shown. Leave one side open and fill the cube with dried peas, beans, or rice. Then very neatly sew up the last side.

Tossed-salad balls

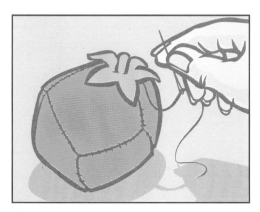

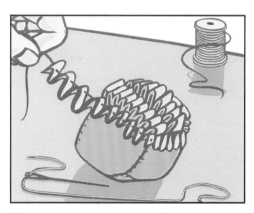

1. To make a tomato juggling ball, make one jolly juggler (see above) using red felt. Cut out a small green star shape and sew it to the top of the juggler as a stem, as shown.

2. For a cucumber, cut two green crescents and two ovals, about 6 in. long and 1½ in. at the widest point. Sew them together, alternating the ovals and crescents.

3. To make a lettuce juggling ball, make a jolly juggler 3 in. by 3 in. using green felt. Cut out extra strips of felt with pinking shears. Gather the strips and sew them onto the juggler, as shown.

AWESOME APRONS

Aprons make good presents as well as being very useful. These two pages show you how to make your own apron and some ways you can decorate it. You can create a special cook's apron with cooking tools, an artist's apron, or a flowery apron for a gardener.

Things you need

½ yard thick cotton fabric
1½ in. x 20 in. bias tape
  or strong, wide ribbon
Pins, needle, and thread
Soft pencil
Fabric pens and paint
Newspaper and masking tape
Fabric glue

Look in the kitchen to get an idea of the tools to paint on your clever cook's apron.

Messy artist's apron

Clever cook's apron

1. To make the paper pattern, draw a rectangle, 16 in. wide by 2 ft. long, on newspaper. Cut it out. Draw two lines, each about 4 in. long, 7 in. from the top of the rectangle.

2. Draw two lines from the two 4 in. lines, straight up to the top of the paper. On one side draw a big curve, as shown. Fold the paper in half lengthwise and cut out the curve.

3. Open the apron pattern. Pin it on the fabric and cut it out. For the pocket, cut a piece of fabric 11 in. wide and 7 in. deep. Turn under and pin the edges. Sew or glue them down.

42

HANDY HINTS

The measurements for the aprons are just a guide. You may want to make your apron bigger or smaller, longer or wider.

Hold a flat sheet of newspaper against you or the person you are making the apron for. Ask someone to help you measure the size you need.

Use fabric paints and puff paints to draw flowers on the busy gardener's apron.

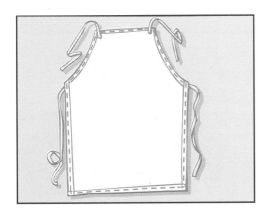

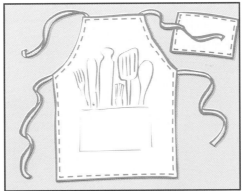

4. Turn under and pin the edges of the apron. Sew or glue them down. Then sew the four cotton tapes in place, at the top and sides of the apron, as shown.

5. Pin the pocket in place and mark it with a pencil. Take it off. Tape the apron to a table and draw some cook's tools with a soft pencil. Make them look as if they are standing in the pocket.

6. Color in the cook's tools with fabric pens and paint. Iron the back of the apron to set the colors. Pin the pocket to the apron and sew it in place, using a neat running stitch.

COZY CHRISTMAS STOCKINGS

On these two pages, you can find out how to make cozy Christmas stockings for the whole family. It is best to use felt as it does not fray and is easy to decorate with sequins, beads, and bits of fabric. As well as making big stockings, try making a string of little ones to hang across the fireplace or in a window.

Things you need

Paper and pencil
Scissors
Large pieces of felt
Large boot or sock
Pins, needle, and thread
Pinking shears
Beads, sequins, buttons,
  scraps of felt, ribbon,
  and sparkles for
  decoration
Thin ribbon
Fabric glue

Super
stocking

Super stocking

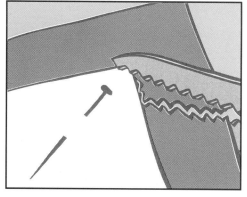

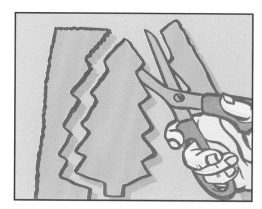

1. Put a big sock or a boot on paper. Draw around it. Take the sock off the paper and cut out the sock pattern, making it a bit bigger all the way around.

2. Pin the paper pattern to a big piece of felt and cut it out with pinking shears. Repeat so that you have two felt sock shapes. These will be your stocking.

3. Draw a big Christmas tree shape on paper. Cut it out, pin the pattern to felt that is a different color than the stocking, and cut out the felt tree. Take out the pins.

Glue different felt pictures on each of your tiny stockings.

HANDY HINTS

Make sure all the decorations you have glued to the stocking are dry before you sew the front to the back. It is best to sew on things like buttons and bows.

You can use another fabric for the stocking, but choose one that does not fray. Cut the edges with pinking shears.

4. Using paper patterns, cut a big pot shape out of felt for the tree to stand in. Then cut present shapes out of different-colored felt, as shown.

5. Spread glue on the back of the tree shape and stick it onto one of the stockings. Glue the pot underneath the tree, and the presents around the pot.

6. Decorate the tree with sequins, sparkles, and felt shapes. Sew the two sides of the stocking together with embroidery thread. Sew a loop of ribbon on the top.

MERRY CHRISTMAS DECORATIONS

These Christmas decorations will make your tree look bright and cheerful and will last for a long time. You can make felt decorations in different shapes, and decorate them with beads, sequins, buttons, and ribbon. Hang the decorations on a tree or give them away as presents.

Things you need

Felt
Batting and thin ribbon
Sparkles, beads, glitter
  glue, and sequins
Scissors or pinking
  shears
Pins, needle, and
  thread
Paper and pencil
Fabric glue

Decorate the front and back of the decorations.

Use gold or silver thread to sew your decorations together.

Sparkling tree

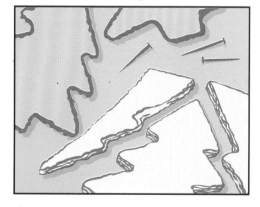

1. Draw a Christmas tree, about 5 in. tall, on paper. Cut it out and pin it to a piece of felt, folded in half. Cut out two felt trees. Cut the same tree shape from a piece of batting.

2. Make a sandwich of the two felt trees with the batting in the middle. Pin them all together and then sew them together, as close to the edges as possible, as shown. Sew on a felt pot.

3. Take out the pins and decorate the tree as if it were a real tree. Sew or glue on beads, sparkles, and strips of sequins. Sew a loop of ribbon on the top of the tree so you can hang it up.

Glitter stocking

Hearts and stars

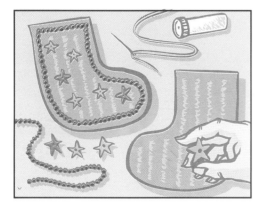

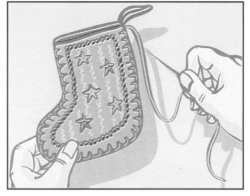

1. Using a paper pattern, cut two Christmas stocking shapes out of felt. Sew or glue a few sequins onto the stockings, leaving the edges free. Decorate the stockings with glitter glue.

2. Sew the two stocking shapes together, as close to the edge as possible. Leave the top open so that you can fill the stocking with tiny presents. Sew a loop of ribbon to the top of the stocking.

Make lots of heart, moon, and star decorations, following the same directions as for the sparkling Christmas tree. Decorate them with strips of sequins, glitter glue, and sparkles.

Sequin stars, hearts, and moons

You can buy sequins in many different shapes and sizes.

HANDY HINTS

To give the decorations pretty edges, cut out the felt shapes with a pair of pinking shears.

Some of these decorations are stuffed with batting to make them nice and thick. Or you can stick two pieces of felt together instead.

If you are not very good at sewing, cover the stitches with beads, braid, or a strip of sequins.

47